MUD BLUE SKY

Marisa Wegrzyn

BROADWAY PLAY PUBLISHING INC
New York
www.broadwayplaypublishing.com
info@broadwayplaypublishing.com

MUD BLUE SKY
© Copyright 2018 Marisa Wegrzyn

Cover art by Debora Roventini

First edition: May 2018
I S B N: 978-0-88145-775-9

Book design: Marie Donovan
Page make-up: Adobe InDesign
Typeface: Palatino

.

MUD BLUE SKY was commissioned by Steppenwolf Theatre, Chicago.

MUD BLUE SKY premiered at Center Stage (Kwame Kwei-Armah, Artistic Director) in Baltimore running from 6 March–14 April 2013. The cast and creative contributors were as follows:

BETH..Susan Rome
SAM...Eva Kaminsky
JONATHAN...Justin Kruger
ANGIE ....Cynthia Darlow

Director...Susanna Gellert
Scenic design.. Neil Patel
Lighting design ....Scott Zielinski
Sound design....................................Victoria (Toy) Delorio
Costume design...Jennifer Moeller
Stage manager..................................Captain Kate Murphy

MUD BLUE SKY was subsequently produced at A Red Orchid Theatre (Kirsten Fitzgerald, Artistic Director) in Chicago running from 17 April–29 June 2014. The cast and creative contributors were as follows:

BETH...Natalie West
SAM...Mierka Girten
JONATHAN... Matt Farabee
ANGIE ....Kirsten Fitzgerald

Director.. Shade Murray
Scenic design.. Jackie Penrod
Lighting design ....Mike Durst
Sound design.................................Brando Triantafillou
Costume design..Karen Kawa
Stage manager.. S G Heller

CHARACTERS & SETTING

BETH, *female, 50s*
SAM, *female, 40s*
JONATHAN, *male, 18*
ANGIE, *female, late 40s/50s*

A hotel room at a chain hotel in Rosemont, IL, near O'Hare Airport.

&

An area behind the hotel. Overgrown, a scraggly oasis of nature under the flight path.

Time: The present. Spring. Night. (52 °F, cloudless.)

Scene One

(Night. A hotel room. Dark. Some illumination from the lights in the parking lot outside. The "burrrzzzzz" of the air conditioning.)

(The door opens: hallway light, a weary female silhouette in the door frame. This is BETH. *She wears a flight attendant's uniform. She wheels a carry-on suitcase.)*

(She enters and the door shuts. It's dark again.)

(She turns on the bathroom light and washes her hands in the bathroom. Sound of shower curtain opening and closing. She turns off the bathroom light. Dark again)

(She goes to the window and looks outside.)

(She stands in the dark.)

(Her cell phone chimes a text message!)

(She types a reply, phone light illuminating her face.)

(Dark again)

(She turns on a light. She looks under the bed.)

(The hotel room phone rings.)

BETH: *(Answers phone:)* Already told you no.
*

No because I mean no, that's the "no" I mean.
*

You know what time we have to be out.
*

Yeah, well.
*

You say that now.

*

Don't come over here. I am going to bed.

*

(Hangs up the phone)

(BETH *finds the T V remote and turns on the T V. Her thumb hits something sticky on the remote. She turns on the lamp to look at what she touched on the remote control. It's a glob of something from a previous room occupant. She goes to the bathroom to wash her hands. There is a knock at the hotel room door. With a towel drying her hands, she opens the door.* SAM *is outside. She wears a flight attendant's uniform, same as* BETH's.)

SAM: A vodka soda, some Pinot Grigio? That horrible scotch you like?

BETH: Tell Gina I send my regrets.

SAM: Tell her that yourself. Gina, did you say "Gina"?

BETH: Yeah. Gina. No?

SAM: Her name is Haley. Gina isn't even close to Haley where'd you get "Gina"?

BETH: She looks like a Gina.

SAM: We're going to Cotters Lounge.

BETH: Cotters Lounge is sticky.

SAM: That's decades of character. Free drinks when what's-his-face bartends Saturday. Guy with the neckbeard. Captain Neckbeard.

BETH: Rick.

SAM: Rick. *Riiiiiick.*

You don't want Cotters Lounge, where do you want? Let's do what you want to do.

Let me tell you where we're going first, we're going to IHOP first. Bacon. Greasy hash browns. Salty encased meat with a satisfying snap.

BETH: My back is wrecked.

SAM: Turn around. Let me see your back.

BETH: Oh, you have X-ray vision, okay.

(BETH's cell phone chimes a text message. She will look at it and type a reply. SAM picks up the T V remote.)

SAM: I'm not saying you're exaggerating your pain, but I know that when I have pain due to the touch of arthritis in my hip, I would drink a drink and eat a pancake.
(Hits the glob of sticky with her thumb)
Uhhhh fuuuuuhh eeeuuuugh.
(She goes to the bathroom)

BETH: There's something on the remote.

SAM: *(Off)* Yeah thanks.
(She returns.)
Let's make Gina's first layover nice before her perky blood clots.

BETH: Thought her name was Haley.

SAM: Aw now you got me messed up on her name.

BETH: She looks like a Gina.

SAM: Well shit. She does look like a Gina. Halley's comet: Haley. That's how I'll remember it. Little Halley's Comet with brand new big girl pants needs her new work-friends in a mean city.

BETH: This isn't the city.

SAM: O'Hare is in the city.
It's a goiter of the city.

(Text chime. SAM looks at her phone)

SAM: Oh great. Great. *(Reads:)* "dishwasher broken"
Great. That's great.
(Typing:)
"W h a t h a p p e n e d ?"

(BETH *will go to the window, look outside, shut the curtain, check her watch, go to her bag to change out of her work clothes*)

SAM: We're meeting Angie at Cotters Lounge.

BETH: Angie? She lives in Chicago now?

SAM: Suburbs, somewhere. La Grange?

BETH: I haven't talked to Angie since, uh. Last time we flew together, before, uh, *(Nods)*

SAM: Fat and fired.

BETH: Well, *(Nods)*

SAM: It is what it is.

BETH: What's Angie up to?

SAM: Moved in with her mom.

BETH: I mean her weight.

SAM: Oh—oh that's mean.

BETH: She moved in with her mom?

SAM: Yeah her mom's not well, suffering from, I don't know, being old. And her divorce went through last month, so. Angie didn't sound good last I talked to her. She hasn't found another job. You know that? Angie is a cautionary tale.

BETH: Great idea going to I-HOP, then.

SAM: I have self-control.

BETH: Not last year.

SAM: That was a thyroid issue.

BETH: All right.

SAM: I don't fluctuate more than two pounds.

BETH: All right.

SAM: Lift me and guess how much I weigh.

BETH: No.

SAM: Or guess first. And then lift me. And guess again.
(She is at the window, opens curtain, looking at her reflection)
Two pounds up or down. My reflection's the same as ever. Come here.

BETH: What?

SAM: Come here.

BETH: Why?

SAM: This kid in the parking lot is wearing a tuxedo.

(BETH looks.)

SAM: I love teenage boys in tuxedos. Like seeing a little dog wear a Halloween costume. I bet that kid is getting lucky on prom night. T.J. is a year off from prom, but if he brought a girl to a hotel on prom night, I would end him. Of course I'd feel relieved a girl wanted to spend more than five minutes with him. Did you get laid on prom night?

BETH: Didn't go to prom.

SAM: Whaaaaat?
Nobody asked you?

BETH: Somebody asked me. Didn't want to go.

SAM: "Didn't want to go." Sure.

My prom night ended in the back of a Buick Le Sabre. Gave my date a blow job. He started crying. "I'm a Mormon!"

BETH: You want to get the cab tomorrow?

SAM: You can get it.

BETH: I was more asking if you would get the cab
tomorrow.

SAM: Then ask.

BETH: Will you get the cab tomorrow?

SAM: Why? It's your turn.

BETH: I'm low on cash.

SAM: I would love to get the cab tomorrow. It's my
favorite thing, getting the cab.

(*Text chime*)

(SAM *looks at her phone*)

SAM: "forks melted."
(*?*)

BETH: Plastic forks in the dishwasher?

SAM: Is there a scenario where silverware would melt?

BETH: Silverware can melt in a house fire.
Ask him if your dishwasher broke in a house fire.

(SAM *looks at* BETH—*that's not funny*)

BETH: Doesn't T.J. usually stay with your mom—?

SAM: Mom needed a break.
This is a trial run.
I mean he's seventeen, so.

BETH: Mm.

(BETH *exits to the bathroom.* SAM *makes a call.*)

SAM: (*On phone:*) Hey.
*

Like plastic forks?
*

Plastic disposable forks?
*

They're *disposable.*
*

I can't get a repair guy this weekend. Wash the dishes by hand.

*

Take a sponge and put dish soap on the sponge.

*

Under the sink.

*

Are you looking under the sink?

*

Move things so you can see other things.

*

Swear to god you will find a sponge if you look.

*

Fine, live in your own filth but the kitchen better be clean when I get home.

*

Wednesday.

*

Love you. …T.J.? …

(She ends the call.)

(A moment alone.)

(BETH enters from the bathroom.)

BETH: Go drink. Go.

SAM: Come on, Beth. I'm going to get shitty and Angie will talk about her dog and Haley who looks like a boring Gina will be boring I mean if she looked like a "fun Gina" it would be different, but she's not a "fun Gina" she's a *Hhhhaley.*

BETH: She's a nice girl.

SAM: Remember Gloria Vilaro? She was fun.

BETH: She did a lot of cocaine.

SAM: Yeah but she was *fun.* Wonder where she is now.

BETH: Cancer.

SAM: What? No.

BETH: Gloria Vilaro yeah.

SAM: What? No. Where'd you hear that?

BETH: Suzanne Walsh.

SAM: Oh fuck her. Someone's gotta know where Gloria
Vilaro is. People like Gloria Vilaro don't get cancer and
disappear.
Suzanne Walsh.

BETH: Suzanne didn't steal your scarf get over it.

SAM: Alan said he saw her wearing it. And she stole
that alcohol.

BETH: You don't know that.

SAM: I know things.
I know things.
You coming or what?
You're not coming.
Fine.
(On her way out.)
Five-thirty.

BETH: Yep.

SAM: I got the cab. Always a pleasure.

BETH: Goodnight, Sam.

SAM: Goodnight, Beth.

BETH: Tell Angie I'm sorry her life is shit.

SAM: She'll probably tell me to tell you the same thing.
(She exits.)

(BETH is alone.)

(She fixes her hair.)

(She puts on a light jacket.)

(She takes a few mini liquor bottles out of her bag, puts them in her jacket pockets with her cell phone and room key. Gets some cash, counts it, puts it in her pocket.)

(She cracks one bottle open, downs it, tosses the bottle in the garbage.)

(She opens the window curtain and looks at the tuxedo kid outside.)

(She gets his attention. Points at her watch. Holds up her hand: "five minutes". She points, gesturing around the back of the hotel.)

(She closes the curtain.)

(Turns off the lights, opens the door, blaze of hallway light, and she's gone.)

Scene Two

(Behind the hotel. A secluded, overgrown area under a landing path.)

(JONATHAN stands there looking up.)

(He wears a tuxedo. His backpack is slung over a shoulder.)

(BETH enters. JONATHAN acknowledges her.)

(Noise of an approaching airplane. They both look up and wait for it. It's loud. It's a huge thing. Then it goes.)

BETH: Haircut.

JONATHAN: Looks stupid.

BETH: It looks good.

JONATHAN: Yeah but it looks stupid. Barber messed it up short.

BETH: If you told me it was prom night I wouldn't've bothered you.

JONATHAN: No big deal.

BETH: Sure?

JONATHAN: No big deal.

BETH: Was it at a, a hotel, or, uh…

JONATHAN: Hilton. In Schaumburg. Near the Ikea Store?

BETH: I bought a bookcase at Ikea two years ago. It's still in the box. There's a pile of books on top of it.

JONATHAN: Was that one of your co-workers? In the window?

BETH: Oh yeah, yeah.

JONATHAN: She was, like, staring at me.

BETH: She thought you looked cute in your tuxedo.

JONATHAN: *(Shrugs)* It's a rental.

BETH: Every man looks great in a tux. James Bond. Who doesn't want to be James Bond? You could shoot Commies.

(JONATHAN *stares at* BETH.)

BETH: Because you look like James Bond, with your *(gestures tux, bow tie).* Commies. Communists.

JONATHAN: I know what a Commie is.

BETH: Oh I guess I was just waiting for your face to do something in recognition of a word.

(Pause. JONATHAN *gets something from his bag)*

JONATHAN: It's fifteen extra.

BETH: Fifteen?

JONATHAN: Yeah.

BETH: You could've mentioned the bump.

JONATHAN: My guy jacked up the really good stuff. You're the only one buys the really good stuff.

BETH: All right.

JONATHAN: It might come back down next time.

BETH: All right.

JONATHAN: Sorry.

BETH: All right.

(BETH *and* JONATHAN *continue talking as she gets her cash. He will hand her a sandwich bag with a joint)*

JONATHAN: Will you be in town next week?

BETH: Yeah.

JONATHAN: Because I—

BETH: Wait. No. I won't (*"Be in town"*) sorry, go ahead.

JONATHAN: No you go.

BETH: Not next week but the next-next week, probably, but there's a chance not. But for sure not next week. I interrupted you.

JONATHAN: If you don't need me next week, doesn't matter.

BETH: If I'm in next-next week I will, uh (*mimes texting*) when I get in.

JONATHAN: Cool.

BETH: Yep.

JONATHAN: See you next-next week.

(JONATHAN'*s leaving.* BETH *stops him with:*)

BETH: Did you have a date for prom tonight, or, uh…?

JONATHAN: Yeah.

BETH: It's only nine o'clock.

JONATHAN: Yeah.

BETH: On prom night.

JONATHAN: Yeah.

(BETH *nods.*)

JONATHAN: There's a Top Chef marathon tonight, so, might go home watch that.

BETH: I haven't caught much of this season.

JONATHAN: Not as good as last season.

BETH: It never is.

(BETH *lights the joint. Inhales.* JONATHAN *takes this as his cue to take off. But she holds out the joint to him.*)

JONATHAN: No thanks.

BETH: I ever tell you how good you roll these?

JONATHAN: No.

(BETH *inhales deeply. She tilts her head back, blows smoke. She remains like that, head back, looking at the sky, for what seems like a long time, like she's preparing to say something poetic.*)

(*Her neck is stuck.*)

JONATHAN: Should I...do something?

BETH: Nope. Fine. I'm fine.
(*Eases her head/neck to normal*)
What happened with your date?

JONATHAN: Nothing.

BETH: Nothing?
(*Beat*)
All right.

(*Pause*)

JONATHAN: She took off with her friends. She was like (*Imitating his date's non-enthusiasm for his company:*) "You can come with us... if you want." I didn't want to hang out with her stupid friends. Her stupid friends are stupid.

(BETH *offers the joint again.* JONATHAN *takes it and smokes, more out of politeness for her offer than wanting to smoke.*

This is the only time he will smoke. He hands the joint back to herh and gets a 20oz bottle of Mountain Dew from his backpack to drink.)

JONATHAN: She was really into my ear.

BETH: What?

JONATHAN: She's just all *(Tongue)* in my ear like *(Tongue)* all over my ear.

BETH: At the dance?

JONATHAN: No no, like, we were at the dance, and it was all sweaty. Well I was all sweaty. I'm still kinda sweaty, look at this. *(Wet shirt pits)*

BETH: Gross.

JONATHAN: There weren't many slow songs, like slow-dance songs. It was a lot of "let's jump around like morons" songs. I was like… "you want to go to my car?" You know?

BETH: Sure.

JONATHAN: And she's like "yeah." So we do. We start, like, making out?

BETH: Go on.

JONATHAN: Her tongue was all *(Tongue gesture, with weird face)* In my ear.

BETH: She made that face?

JONATHAN: What?

BETH: That face. *(Imitates his weird face)* That— nevermind—she stuck her wet, hot slug of a tongue in your ear.

JONATHAN: Like, how weird is that?

BETH: How deep did she go? Was she tasting wax?

JONATHAN: Is that something girls do?

BETH: There are all kinds of people.

(Pause)

Do you like her?

(JONATHAN *shrugs, affirmative.*)

BETH: After her tongue probed your ear and she ditched you, you like her. Lemmie guess. She's pretty.

JONATHAN: Amazingly pretty. It's not just me thinks that. Like, even pretty people think she's pretty.

BETH: Other than you find her attractive, you would say, overall, it was a negative experience.

JONATHAN: Yeah.

BETH: Think about that.

Are you thinking about it?

JONATHAN: Yeah.
She's hot.

BETH: Imagine you lost your sight and you didn't know what this girl looks like.

JONATHAN: She's really hot.

BETH: Forget that.

JONATHAN: I can't forget it she's really hot.

BETH: Pretend you don't know how hot she is because you are blind.

JONATHAN: Why am I blind?

BETH: Pretend.

JONATHAN: I'd like to know the circumstance of my handicap.

BETH: *(After a thought)* You are blind because chemicals exploded in your face and the emergency shower in the lab didn't work.

JONATHAN: *(Thinks, nods)* Did the chemicals turn me into a mutant? Like X-Men.

BETH: This isn't a superhero fantasy, Jonathan. This is a serious hypothetical situation and I would like you to treat it accordingly seriously serious. I ever tell you I met Stevie Wonder?

JONATHAN: No.

BETH: I met Stevie Wonder on a flight.

JONATHAN: Okay.

BETH: And he's blind. And he's great. Got his autograph. The girls were all, "Don't do it. He's blind".

JONATHAN: Was he nice?

BETH: Gracious.

JONATHAN: Good autograph?

BETH: Indecipherable.

This girl. Who ditched you at prom.

JONATHAN: Molly.

BETH: This girl Molly. What do you like about this Molly?

JONATHAN: She has really great…
(Gestures "boobs")

BETH: Personality?

(JONATHAN shrugs.)

BETH: I do not like this Molly. She was a bad date. You'll have many dates in your life and one of them will be worse than that one. So the bright side is you haven't hit rock bottom.

JONATHAN: Oh, good.

BETH: Fuck.

JONATHAN: What?

BETH: My back.

JONATHAN: You hurt your back?

BETH: Yes.

JONATHAN: Doing what?

BETH: Standing here.

JONATHAN: You hurt your back standing doing nothing?

BETH: Yes.

JONATHAN: Don't you think you should see a doctor or something?

BETH: Anything I do, it won't get better. It won't heal. So I can get surgery and have it heal, maybe. Or…I can just wait until I die. And then my back problem's solved.

JONATHAN: You should talk to a doctor.

BETH: You should talk to a doctor have him check out your sweaty pits. Rental place is gonna charge extra to wring out your shirt. Can I have a sip?
(Mountain Dew)

*(*JONATHAN *gives* BETH *the bottle.)*

BETH: Thanks.
(She'll hold on to the bottle, finish it off)
When're you off to college? You got into Caltech. Caltech, right, you said that last time?

JONATHAN: I don't want to go.

BETH: Then don't.

JONATHAN: My dad said I'd be making a big mistake if I didn't go.

BETH: Like, you're going to regret it if you don't, or, what?

JONATHAN: Yeah, that I'll regret it.

BETH: How would he know? Has he traveled to the future in a time machine? Jumped into the future to talk to your future self, living in a cardboard box because you didn't go to Caltech? Come on. Your dad is an idiot.

JONATHAN: *(Firm)* He's not an idiot.

BETH: Most advice from your elders is pernicious, posturing, bullshit. What seems like wisdom-through-life-experience is the Furniture Store front to a speakeasy of selfish regret. Swilling the bathtub gin of self-loathing. Here's my advice: don't listen to anybody, ever.

JONATHAN: Including you?

BETH: You should listen to me. I'm talking other people.

JONATHAN: Did you go to college?

BETH: Two years.

JONATHAN: You quit?

BETH: I stopped going.

JONATHAN: So you quit.

BETH: I stopped going.

JONATHAN: So…you quit.

BETH: No.

JONATHAN: It seems pretty much the same thing.

BETH: Quitting is stopping but stopping is not quitting. It's just stopping. It's not a decision. It's just running out of, uh.
(Makes vague gesture relating to "momentum")
You throw something up in the air, it comes back down.
(Throws the empty Mountain Dew bottle in the air) What is that?

JONATHAN: Littering.

BETH: It doesn't decide to come back down, it just does. It doesn't quit going up in the air. It stops. It stops and comes back down because it has to. Laws of physics. You learn these things, Jonathan, you will learn these things in college. My boyfriend in college learned to open a beer bottle with his teeth and then learned the school dental plan wasn't very good. And you will learn linguistic distinctions, that which separates one word from another word like quitting and stopping. Like, I'm not quitting my job, I'm retiring which is stopping. Quitting is a neighbor of stopping, it's the neighbor who's stealing the Rolling Stone out of your mailbox while you're out of town that fucking asshole neighbor, fuck him.

JONATHAN: You're retiring? Like, from flying, forever?

(A moment. First time BETH's *told someone she's retiring)*

BETH: Round of layoffs coming up, end of the year. Senior staff have an option to take early retirement. It's a good package. Well. It's a package. The word "good" is subjective.

JONATHAN: You won't be coming through town anymore?

BETH: No.

JONATHAN: Oh.

What will you do after you quit?

BETH: Not "quit".

JONATHAN: What will you do after you stop?

BETH: Umm.

I don't know. I just know I can't, uh.

You know.

I was thinking…

This is stupid, but.

Nevermind.

JONATHAN: What?

BETH: I'd like to start a brewery. Microbrewery. Craft beer. Start a craft beer business out of a garage. And then move to a bigger garage when it gets going. Sounds stupid I say it out loud.

JONATHAN: Why's it stupid?

BETH: "Liking beer" isn't a business plan.

JONATHAN: I'll design the labels for your bottles.

BETH: You draw?

(JONATHAN *gets a sketchbook from his backpack.* BETH *studies one of his illustrations*)

BETH: Ever hear a Wally Wood?

JONATHAN: Yeah. Well no. I know the name.

BETH: He illustrated sci-fi for E C Comics in the 50s.

JONATHAN: Oh right yeah yeah.

BETH: Space squids. Robots. Lost kingdoms of Amazonian vampire women. My older brother was into comic books. Very protective of his collection.
(Fondly)
"Don't touch my stuff, Beth, I'll rip your arm off and beat you with it." I'd read 'em. Memorize exactly how he had left them piled on the stack so he wouldn't know. Anyway. Your drawing reminds me of Wally Wood comics. These tentacles are gorgeous.

(BETH *flips deeper into the sketchbook, finds naked lady sketches*)

JONATHAN: Oh uh that's other stuff.

BETH: You really know how to capture a woman's personality.

JONATHAN: I forgot that was, uh, sorry sorry.

BETH: That's okay.

JONATHAN: Sorry.

BETH: They're good.

(JONATHAN *takes back the sketchbook and puts it in his bag*)

JONATHAN: Can I ask you something?

BETH: Hm.

JONATHAN: Where do you live?

BETH: Why?

JONATHAN: I was just, like, curious. If you're retiring. And you won't be coming back here. Like, if you lived in Los Angeles, and if I was going to Cal Tech and if you needed pot.

BETH: I won't need you.

(*Pause*)

JONATHAN: Let's settle up.

BETH: Settle up. Settle up what settle up?

JONATHAN: You owe me twenty dollars.

BETH: Excuse me?

JONATHAN: Month ago when you didn't have cash.

BETH: I paid you fifty.

JONATHAN: Wh—? When?

BETH: Last time. Or the time before last time.

JONATHAN: No you didn't.

BETH: I paid you fifty. I had a fifty you couldn't break, I said this'll cover that. Probably should've covered this time now that I think about it.

JONATHAN: You didn't give me fifty last time.

BETH: I did so.

JONATHAN: Last time I brought it up you didn't have cash. I said "okay". You said "next time".

BETH: You're just saying stuff.

JONATHAN: This is next time. This, right now, is next time. If it's the last time I don't want to be out twenty bucks.

BETH: I paid you. It was that time I brought you Cinnabon. I brought you Cinnabon from Terminal 2. You ever been in Terminal 2? That's budget airlines, it's a third world country.

JONATHAN: Maybe you forgot.

BETH: Don't—don't get in the habit a telling a person they forgot, like you read their mind, like you know what they're thinking like you're a mind reader? Are you a mind reader? Are you a mind reader?

JONATHAN: No.

BETH: You don't know anything 'cause you're not a mind reader.

JONATHAN: You owe me twenty bucks.

BETH: I'll give you twenty. I do not *owe* you.

JONATHAN: If you don't think you owe it, I don't want it.

BETH: Oh, now you don't want it, Uncle Pennybags? I am giving it to you.

JONATHAN: I don't want it.

BETH: You're gonna take it.

JONATHAN: I don't want it.

BETH: You're gonna take my money and whether or not you're gonna be a big crybaby about it is up to you.

JONATHAN: Oh, fuck you.

BETH: Fuck me? Fuck you.

JONATHAN: Fuck off.

BETH: You fuck off. Probably fleeced me / / on the extra fifteen for the good stuff.

JONATHAN: *(//Overlap above)* Forget it. Goodnight. Goodbye.

BETH: Where are you going?

JONATHAN: Don't treat me like a jerk.

BETH: Not treating you like a jerk, I'm treating you like a liar.

JONATHAN: *(Leaving)* I'm not a liar.

BETH: Oh come on, I'm just—okay—wait—Jonathan.

(JONATHAN *stops.*)

BETH: There is a chance I was mistaken about our financial situation and you are right and I said I'll pay you the twenty now I'll pay you the twenty. I have a subjectively good early retirement.
(Checks pockets)
I don't have any cash.
It's up in my room.
Come on.

(JONATHAN *doesn't move*)

BETH: I do not want to walk back down here I am not coming back down You want your money, you come up and we'll be done Either you want your twenty bucks or you don't.
Up to you.
I don't give a shit.
(She stumbles into the dark.)

JONATHAN: You're going the wrong way.

(BETH *re-enters as if she's going to confront* JONATHAN *on this fact. She realizes he is correct, then re-exits toward the hotel. He follows her)*

Scene Three

(BETH's hotel room. Dark)

(The door opens.)

(Hallway light. BETH's silhouette in the door frame. She enters.)

(Then JONATHAN's silhouette in the door. He enters.)

(The door shuts.)

(It's dark again.)

(BETH turns on the bathroom light and washes her hands in the bathroom and wets a washcloth in the sink. She turns off the bathroom light.)

(Dark again)

(BETH turns on the light. JONATHAN stays near the door.)

(BETH goes to the bed. Folds back the covers. She is particular and careful about how she undoes a bed.)

(She flops down on the bed and she puts the folded wet washcloth over her eyes.)

(It seems she's forgotten about him.)

BETH: Bring me my bag.

(JONATHAN does. BETH takes her wallet out. Her eyes still covered with the washcloth, she takes a bill out for him.)

JONATHAN: That's a one.

(BETH takes another bill out)

JONATHAN: That's a one.

(Another)

JONATHAN: That's a one.

(Another)

JONATHAN: That's a five.

(Another)

JONATHAN: That's a one.

(Another)

JONATHAN: That's a one.

(Another)

JONATHAN: That's a one.

(Another)

JONATHAN: That's a receipt.

BETH: For what?

JONATHAN: Hudson News.

(BETH *takes back the receipt. Finally looks in her wallet.)*

BETH: How much is that?

JONATHAN: Eleven dollars.

BETH: I'll get you nine dollars.
(She makes no effort to do so, closes her eyes again)

JONATHAN: Somebody drew on George Washington and turned him into Batman. How cool would it have been if the first president of the United States was Batman?
(He gets the remote.)
You get Bravo?

BETH: Some hotels get Bravo some don't. I forget if this is a Bravo hotel. I don't know where I am.

(JONATHAN *touches the glob on the remote as he turns on the T V)*

JONATHAN: Ewww sick. Something on the remote.

BETH: Oh yeah there's something on the remote.

JONATHAN: Sick.

(He goes to the bathroom.)

BETH: The world is a filthy place. You should see what people do on airplanes. Snotty Kleenex in the seatback

pocket, gum on the armrests. Sometimes have to close
a toilet for a mess of foul explosion, and the smell. The
smell. You don't want to know. This one guy last week,
just, diarreah everywhere. I don't want to talk about it.
This woman put a soiled baby diaper in the seatback
pocket. Don't ever stick your hand in a seatback
pocket. You'll be very sorry.

(JONATHAN *returns with the remote, wiped clean. Flips
channels)*

JONATHAN: You don't have Bravo.

BETH: I think this hotel has Bravo. I think this is a Bravo
hotel.

JONATHAN: What time do you have to go to work
tomorrow?

BETH: Early.

JONATHAN: How early's early?

BETH: Four. No five-thirty. Today's Saturday right?

JONATHAN: Yeah.

BETH: Five-thirty.

JONATHAN: How do you wake up so early.

BETH: Step one: set the alarm twelve minutes before
you have to get out of bed. That allows for three hits
on an Indigo travel alarm snooze button, four minutes
each snooze. Step two: get out of bed because you
fucking have to. Step three: there is no step three.

JONATHAN: My snooze button is nine minutes.

BETH: Travel clocks have a shorter snooze because
they're smaller so there's less snooze that fits inside.

JONATHAN: Get a clock with a longer snooze.

BETH: Why?

JONATHAN: So you can sleep longer.

BETH: I'm a morning person. Booze'll get me but I'm not boozed. And if I get that boozed I chuck it in the shower. Best life advice I can give you: Morning shower puke.

JONATHAN: My dad drinks a lot too.

BETH: I don't drink a lot.

JONATHAN: They got Pay-Per-View.

BETH: Not a lot a lot.

JONATHAN: Wanna watch a movie? Beth?

BETH: Mm.

JONATHAN: You wanna watch a movie?
I'll pay you back for the movie.
Beth? Are you asleep?

(BETH *is asleep.* JONATHAN *makes sure she's asleep. Then buys a pay per view movie.)*

(There's a knock at the door. BETH *wakes. Looks at* JONATHAN)

BETH: You're still here.
(She closes her eyes again.)

(At the door: Knock knock knock)

(BETH *opens her eyes. She leaps out of bed, goes to the door. Looks out the peep hole. Looks at* JONATHAN.)

BETH: You need to go.

JONATHAN: Uh—okay. Like, I should leave?

BETH: Yeah.

JONATHAN: Like leave out the door somebody's knocking on?

BETH: Do the windows open?

JONATHAN: You want me to go out the window?

BETH: Is that all right?

JONATHAN: We're on the second floor.

BETH: You could jump that.

JONATHAN: No I couldn't.

(Knock knock knock)

BETH: Go in the bathroom.

JONATHAN: Is somebody in the hall with a gun?

BETH: No, just go in the bathroom.

JONATHAN: To hide from somebody in the hall with a gun?

BETH: No.

JONATHAN: This feels like right before someone with a gun shoots everybody in the room.

BETH: There's nobody with a gun will you please get in the bathroom please?

(JONATHAN goes into the bathroom, shuts the door.)

(Knock knock knock)

SAM: Beth?

BETH: Ah save your knuckles!
(She looks in the mirror, rubs her eyes. Gets some eyedrops from her bag.)

SAM: Come on.

BETH: Hold on!

(BETH squirts eyedrops and misses. Eyedrops all over her face. BETH opens the door. SAM is there.)

BETH: What?

SAM: Are you asleep?

BETH: Yes.

SAM: Are you crying?

BETH: Allergies. What? What do you want?

SAM: Angie's in m—

(BETH *is blocking* SAM's *entrance.*)

SAM: May I come in? Thank you.

Angie is in my room. I don't know what to do with her.

BETH: What happened to Cotters Lounge?

(JONATHAN's *backpack is still out in the room.* BETH *will find an opportunity to kick it under the bed.*)

SAM: The new girl doesn't drink. Can you believe that? I told her: get a Coke. She said "I don't drink caffeine or sugar." We went to IHOP but she can't eat dairy. Or gluten. How is she even alive? I feel sorry for people who deprive themselves of substance.

BETH: It's a medical condition.

SAM: It's psychosomatic.

BETH: Well. No, // it's celiac disease, but, go on.

SAM: (*Overlap above @ //*) So I inhale pancakes and bacon like a champ. You missed out. We leave the IHOP and Gina didn't want to go drink—

BETH: Haley.

SAM: Shit. Halley's Comet. —After Haley didn't want to go drink, Angie's like "I'll give you a ride back to the hotel." I'm polite, so I say to Angie, "come up to my room for a little." Because I think she'll say "no, no, you're out early tomorrow". You know what she says, she says: "I have a bottle of cognac in my trunk." And there it is, in the trunk, half full bottle of cognac nuzzled up to the spare tire and bag of kitty litter. So Angie is in my room spooning a bottle of cognac, looking for a Top Chef marathon. She's probably wondering why it's taking me fifteen minutes to run down the hall to get Pepto from you.

BETH: Do you need Pepto, really?

SAM: God I love IHOP but I'm going to be crop dusting the aisle tomorrow. I heard a great joke tonight. You wanna hear it?

BETH: Eh.

SAM: You hear the one about the flight attendant who reeks of pot? Because she's in this room and she's you.

(Beat)

BETH: That's not a very good joke.

SAM: Uh huh.

BETH: Here's a good joke how many Germans does it take to change a lightbulb.

SAM: How many. Oh god, is this a Holocaust joke?

BETH: No.

SAM: How many.

BETH: Just one.
(Thinks)
I forgot the punch line.

SAM: You're stoned.

BETH: I'm *fine*.

SAM: Uh huh. Who's the guy?

BETH: What guy?

SAM: Your pot guy.

BETH: I don't have a pot guy.

SAM: You have to have a guy. It's not like you can haul marijuana through the airport. You got a guy. Here.

(BETH looks around—)

SAM: In Chicago. Gloria Vilaro had that guy before she moved on to the blow, and banging every baggage handler in Houston, god bless her, but she also had a pot guy.

BETH: *(Remembering)* Germans are efficient and not very funny.

SAM: All right. I'm not going to pry. Your life is your life. If this is what you need to be your Zen master self at thirty thousand feet, well, fine. Good for you. But I want you to know: it's a burden knowing that people I care about are behaving badly, not that I'm judging you. I am not, as T.J. says, Judgy McJudge-a-lot.
(She looks at the TV)
What are you *watching*?

(For the first time, BETH and SAM both notice the TV which had been on a low volume. The pay-per-view movie JONATHAN ordered is an adult movie.)

(A pause)

BETH: I am watching porn.

SAM: Why?

BETH: I like it.

SAM: Did you order this on the, uh?

BETH: Yep.

SAM: I didn't know you were into this.

BETH: There's a lot you don't know. I also enjoy documentaries about surfing.

(BETH and SAM watch porn.)

SAM: Oh god. Oh! This is filthy.
How much did this cost?

BETH: I don't know. Can I borrow nine dollars?

SAM: What—for this?

BETH: No no for…stuff. I might want a snack tonight some Doritos or uh…
(Distracted by the TV)

(BETH and SAM watch porn)

SAM: You can tell that girl was a gymnast before the implants.

BETH: How do you know?

SAM: Her thighs, you have to train for that position. I did gymnastics in high school. Balance beam.

(BETH *and* SAM *watch porn*)

SAM: I caught T.J. watching porn on his computer. Walked in and he changed the page. Like it makes any sense masturbating to a blank Google search.
(Pause)
My son hates me.

BETH: That's not true.

SAM: You don't know T.J.

BETH: Yeah I do I met him.
That time we went for dinner at that, uh, restaurant with the Skillet Cookie.

SAM: That was *five years ago*. T.J. was a boy. He mutated. Into a brooding, hunched, Boy-Man animal. I just, I don't know.
I'm never there.
You're lucky. You don't have a broken dishwasher to deal with when you get home.
(She heads to the bathroom)

BETH: Wait!

SAM: What?

BETH: Where are you going?

SAM: Bathroom.

BETH: Uh. Uh. Uhhhh.

SAM: Are you having a stroke?

BETH: Toilet's not working.

SAM: Did you call the front desk?

(BETH *thinks*)

SAM: Call the front desk.

(SAM *goes into the bathroom, flushes toilet. She enters, gestures to the flush noise: "works fine"*)

BETH: I, yeah, I don't know. It was acting funny.

(SAM *shuts the bathroom door.* BETH *listens at the door.*)

BETH: Sam?

SAM: What?

BETH: Nothing.

(*Flush sound. Hand washing.* SAM *exits.* BETH *quickly peeks into the bathroom. Where'd* JONATHAN *go?*)

BETH: You won't say anything. About, uh.

SAM: I won't say anything to anyone who might ask you to pee in a cup.

BETH: Thank you.

SAM: You got any more?

BETH: Any more… ?

SAM: Pot, any more pot?

BETH: Why?

(SAM *shrugs.*)

BETH: You should go…
(*Gestures "back to your room"*)

SAM: Lemmie call my room.

BETH: Wh— no. No no no.

SAM: Angie'll bring the fancy cognac, we'll have a drink, catch up.
(*Looking at T V*)
Oh look. Anal.

(BETH *turns off the T V.*)

BETH: I'd really like to sleep now.

(JONATHAN's *cell phone rings in his backpack under the bed.* BETH *and* SAM *both hear the phone.* JONATHAN *comes out of the bathroom.*)

JONATHAN: Uh, hey. Sorry, I have to answer that. Sorry. Where's my, uh.

(BETH *points to under the bed*)

JONATHAN: Thanks. Sorry. Hi.
(He takes his phone out of his backpack.)

JONATHAN: *(Answers phone:)* Molly? Hey. What's up?
(He goes into the bathroom, shuts the door.)

(Off SAM's *look:)*

BETH: I should call Housekeeping about that.

SAM: The tuxedo kid. What's he doing here?

BETH: I invited him.

SAM: To watch porn?

BETH: What? No.

SAM: You were watching porn with a child.

BETH: I fell asleep and he ordered this on the thing.

SAM: You were in bed with a child and you fell asleep and he ordered porn.

BETH: You're making this something it's not.

SAM: All right.

BETH: This is not a big deal. But if you'd not mention… in addition to the other thing you'd not mention… this…
(Gestures to the bathroom)
Not to Becky, not to Carol, especially not to Alan because I will never hear the end of it from him. Okay? I'd. Appreciate it. Okay?

SAM: This young man is your pot guy?

(Off BETH's *look:)*

SAM: I knew you had a pot guy! I knew it! Pot guy
hiding in your bathroom!
Oh my god.
He was hiding in the bathroom when I was—!

BETH: Must've been behind the, uh…

SAM: What if he'd been behind the shower curtain
listening to me do my business and…y'know
(Gestures "jerking off")

BETH: Jonathan's a nice kid.

SAM: Nice kids do this—
(Gesture again)
—too.

BETH: I owed Jonathan cash for the pot, he came up to
my room to get it. That's all that happened. So. Not a
word.

SAM: Not a word.
(Smiles)

BETH: Swear to god, Sam.

SAM: He's a cute little thing in his tuxedo, in't he?
(She picks up his backpack, opens it)
With his little backpack and everything.

BETH: Don't—don't do that.

SAM: It was already open-ish.
(She takes out a condom)
Ahh, to be young and awkwardly groping.

BETH: Sam.

SAM: Okay okay okay.
*(She returns the condoms to the bag and removes a sheathed
hunting knife)*

He carries a knife. What kind of kid carries a knife?
This kind of kid hides in the shower: *("Psycho" stab
gesture)*

BETH: Put it back.

*(*SAM *takes out a book. Shows* BETH*)*

BETH: *Pride & Prejudice.*

*(*JONATHAN *enters from the bathroom.* SAM *returns the
knife to the backpack.)*

JONATHAN: I have it just in case.

SAM: *Pride & Prejudice?*

JONATHAN: That's my mom's.

*(*SAM *returns the items to the bag.* JONATHAN *puts his
phone away in the bag.)*

JONATHAN: Thanks for picking up my stuff. It must
have spilled all over the place for no reason.

BETH: Jonathan, this is Sam. We work together.

*(*JONATHAN *and* SAM *shake hands.)*

JONATHAN: Saw you before.

SAM: Oh, I know.

JONATHAN: In the window. You were staring at me.

SAM: Oh yes, you mean in the window. I was the
creepy one then.

JONATHAN: I didn't want to scare you, or, uh, sorry.

SAM: Forget it happened.
My son's about your age. Looking at colleges.
Missouri, Boulder, Tulane. Are you doing the college
thing?

JONATHAN: Caltech. Maybe.

SAM: Oh wow. You got in to Caltech?

JONATHAN: Yeah.

SAM: Wow. That's impressive. Tough school to get in to.

JONATHAN: I guess.

SAM: I don't think T.J. can get in there. He's smart, but he doesn't study. More into playing video games and avoiding responsibility. He'll major in that. Heck, he already has his PhD in that. I like your tuxedo.

JONATHAN: It's a rental.

SAM: Prom night.

JONATHAN: Yeah.

SAM: We were talking about prom earlier.

BETH: Sam frightened a Mormon on prom night.

SAM: I didn't frighten him. I solidified his faith. Was Beth a good prom date?

JONATHAN: Maybe I should go.

SAM: I'm teasing! Teasing. Did you have a date?

JONATHAN: She, like. Went off with her friends.

SAM: She ditched you?

(SAM *looks to* BETH *who nods yes.*)

SAM: What a bitch.

BETH: I don't really like her either.

JONATHAN: That was her just called. Her group kinda broke up for the night and she wanted to know what I was up to. If I wanted to hang out, watch a movie or something.

SAM: Did she apologize for ditching you?

JONATHAN: (*Thinks*) No.

SAM: You need a drink.
(*She goes to the phone.*)

BETH: He's under age.

SAM: He's *your pot dealer*. It's prom night.

BETH: Don't call Angie over.

SAM: Angie would love to see you. Half hour tops, and you don't even have to go anywhere.
(To JONATHAN*)*
Nightcap?
(She dials.)

BETH: You don't have to stay.

JONATHAN: If you don't want me to stay I won't stay.

BETH: I didn't say I didn't want you to stay.

JONATHAN: Do you want me to stay?

BETH: It's your prom night. You should be with your prom date.

JONATHAN: You said she was a bad date.

SAM: What are you getting dating advice from Beth for? Hold on.

(On phone:)
Angie, hey, I'm in Beth's room.
*
Yeah.
*
It's not a Bravo hotel.
*
I thought it was too but it's not.
*
208. You know, hey, why not bring the bottle of cognac? Great.
(Hangs up the phone)
Of course, you don't have to stay. Your former prom date is desperate and alone and is making a last ditch effort to salvage the baggage in the burning wreckage of the evening. Why go back to her and give her the satisfaction?

JONATHAN: Because she's hot.

SAM: She can't be that hot.

(JONATHAN *gets his cell phone.*)

BETH: You don't want to regret not having a prom night.

SAM: This one would know something about that. Nobody asked her.

BETH: Somebody asked me. I didn't go. I didn't want to go.

SAM: Why not?

BETH: I didn't have a dress. (*To* JONATHAN) If you want to go see your prom date, you should go.

SAM: You are better than to go crawling back to a girl who doesn't want you.

(JONATHAN *shows* SAM *a pic on his phone.*)

SAM: How'd you get a girl so hot, you sly dog?

(*There's a knock at the door.*)

(SAM *opens the door.* ANGIE *is there with an expensive bottle of Remy Martin cognac, and a couple extra plastic-wrapped plastic cups.* ANGIE *is not fashionable, but has made an effort to look nice tonight. Maybe she's not fat, but she's heavier than an average flight attendant.*)

ANGIE: I brought cups if you didn't have cups. Hi Beth!

BETH: Hey Angie, come on in!

ANGIE: Oh my gosh, look at you. It's great to see you. It's really great.

BETH: You too, yeah. You look good.

ANGIE: Oh. Thanks. Thanks.

BETH: It's good to see you. It's, been, god.

ANGIE: Over two years now.

BETH: I was trying to remember the last time.

ANGIE: Christmas. We flew together that Christmas flight.

BETH: Oh right, right.

ANGIE: That was actually my last flight. Had the rest of the holiday off, and then, well.

BETH: Yeah.

ANGIE: I have some, uh.

(ANGIE *gives* BETH *the bottle.*)

BETH: Oh, excellent, thanks.

SAM: I like your shoes.

ANGIE: They're new!

SAM: Super cute!

ANGIE: I ordered them online.

SAM: Zappos?

ANGIE: Yeah, they have the free return shipping if things don't fit. Or if you don't like what you bought. Shipping is free.
(*She notices* JONATHAN.)
Hello.

JONATHAN: Hi.

BETH: Jonathan, Angie. Angie, Jonathan. We used to fly together.

SAM: They were in the same training class.

ANGIE: Roommates during training, ages ago.

BETH: (*Looking at bottle*) You sure you want to waste this on us?

ANGIE: What do you mean?

BETH: It's a really good bottle of cognac.

ANGIE: Well.

SAM: How good a bottle?

ANGIE: Oh, I don't know.

BETH: Couple hundred dollars at least.

ANGIE: Four hundred.

SAM: No way. Come on.

ANGIE: It's a special night seeing you again. I thought…it would be nice.

SAM: Well, darn it if I pass up a four hundred dollar bottle of cognac.

ANGIE: *(To* JONATHAN*)* You're friends with Beth?

SAM: Jonathan's her drug dealer.

ANGIE: Oh! What kind of drugs?

SAM: Pot.

ANGIE: Ohhh. Been a long time since I…
(Nods)

BETH: Really?

ANGIE: Oh yeah! I did it for a little. It was not for me. I got tired of never being able to remember where I put things. Like one time I lost my entire car for two weeks. Found it parked in the lot of a strip mall with a firing range. I like your tuxedo.

JONATHAN: Thanks.

ANGIE: You look very James Bond.

BETH: Yeah he's gonna shoot some Commies later. *(Silence)* James Bond, Commies, Commu—forget it.

SAM: *(Offering a pour)* Beth?

BETH: Two fingers.

SAM: How 'bout one finger.
(Flips the bird)

Ha ha.

BETH: How 'bout go fuck yourself.

SAM: You wish. Want some?

JONATHAN: Yeah.

SAM: You ever had cognac?

JONATHAN: *(Lies)* Sure.

SAM: Suuuuure. High roller.

BETH: Would you just—
(Gestures "give him some")

(SAM pours cognac for JONATHAN.)

ANGIE: How do you two know each other?

SAM: Was wondering the same thing.

JONATHAN: We met at the airport.

BETH: Denver.

JONATHAN: There was this dog.

BETH: You know Greg in Denver, on security? Kinda stocky, mustache. Sweet guy, not always on-the-ball, likes to whistle?

SAM: Kinda flirty?

BETH: You know it. Asked me to go for a drink when I'm on Denver layover. I say, "Ask me next time." "Ask me next time" "Ask me next time, Greg". So Greg has this drug dog, Gertie.

SAM: Wait sorry. Can we pause? You got a dollar for a soda? I can't drink cognac neat.

BETH: No no no.

SAM: What?

BETH: You don't pour soda in cognac.

SAM: I do.

BETH: Well you're wrong.

SAM: I can't drink it neat. It tastes like a mummy on fire.

BETH: Angie brings an expensive cognac and you want to ruin it.

SAM: Angie? Do you mind?

ANGIE: It's all right.

SAM: See, there we go, who has a dollar?

JONATHAN: I have a dollar.

SAM: Jonathan has a dollar! What a gentleman. True gentleman would offer to hoof it to the machine grab the soda as well.

JONATHAN: What kind of soda do you want?

SAM: 7-Up, but if it's not 7-Up, then Sprite. But not Sierra Mist. If there's only Sierra Mist, then get me a Coke, but if all they got's Pepsi, then get me a Sierra Mist. To the right end of the hall. And! —The ice bucket.

Thanks, sweetie.

(JONATHAN *exits the room with the ice bucket.*)

SAM: He's like a little butler.

BETH: Don't be doing that.

SAM: Doing what?

BETH: If anybody's going to send him to fetch things, it should be me.

SAM: He offered to pay for the soda.

BETH: To pay for it, not be your little servant.

ANGIE: Why is he wearing a tuxedo?

BETH & SAM: Prom.

ANGIE: He's in high school???

SAM: Beth likes 'em young.

BETH: Be nice, okay? Don't be a shitty person.

SAM: Shitty person?
(*To* ANGIE)
Was I a shitty person?

ANGIE: Suppose it depends on what you mean by shitty person.

SAM: Beth: define "shitty person."

BETH: You're selfish.

SAM: *Everybody* is selfish. Is *everybody* shitty?

BETH: You force people to walk backwards on the cart.

SAM: Wha—you *take* the backwards side.

BETH: I, no.

SAM: You're there first, you *take* it.

BETH: Because I'm efficient on the beverage cart I'm stuck walking backwards.

SAM: You pull out the cart. You're on that side. There are only two sides.

BETH: I do not like always having my backside stared at.

SAM: Don't think about it. Shut it out. Who cares about your ass?

BETH: I care, when the grey suits in Business Class get loose and grabby.

SAM: You know the phrase "benefit of the doubt."
That, yes, tight quarters lead to an accidental touch?
Or that, maybe, you think I'm a shitty person and I'm intentionally trying to irritate you when, maybe, in fact, I had no idea that you thought I was being selfish, or that I was aware that I was being selfish. You are good at your job and you get to the cart first and that's

all I thought it was. Or this young man offers to go
to the vending machine and buy me 7-Up and I let
him do it because it's a nice, thoughtful gesture on his
part. But it's good to know that you think I'm a shitty
person. I appreciate knowing how you perceive me. It's
a gift to know what people think about you.

BETH: I'm just saying…

SAM: You want me to walk backwards on the beverage
cart more is what you're saying.

BETH: Or at least offer to walk backwards.

SAM: All right.

(JONATHAN *enters with a bottle of Sprite and a full ice
bucket)*

JONATHAN: The machine on this floor was Sierra Mist
but the machine on the third floor was Sprite.

SAM: He went upstairs! The extra mile. Thank you.

JONATHAN: Weird though.

SAM: What's weird.

JONATHAN: That there's two different brands of lemon-
lime soda in one hotel.

SAM: Super weird, mystery of the universe. Okay, let's
unpause to hear the story of your meet-cute.

(SAM *opens the Sprite and it sprays everywhere. Stunned.*
BETH *and* ANGIE *laugh.)*

SAM: *(To* JONATHAN*)* Did you shake it up?

JONATHAN: No. The bottle shakes up when it drops in
the machine. You have to open it slowly.

SAM: I know how to open a soda bottle.
It's not funny. It's not funny.

BETH: Yes it is.

ANGIE: Your face was like—(*Imitates Sam's surprised faced*) Oh god it feels good to laugh. I feel like I ran a marathon.

SAM: Most exercise you've gotten in two years, probably.

(BETH *is still laughing at* SAM.)

SAM: Well ha ha, motherfucker, you get to sleep on Sprite-soaked pillows tonight.
(*She splashes Sprite across the pillows on the bed*)

BETH: What the hell, Sam?

SAM: Not so funny now, huh.

BETH: I have to sleep here.

SAM: It was an accident. Spills happen all the time. Who knows what's been spilled in this bed.
(*She picks up the hotel phone, hits the housekeeping button.*)
Little buddy shook up a soda that exploded all over *me*, but you have every right to be pissed.

BETH: He said he didn't shake it.

SAM: (*On phone*) Hi, can I get two pillows for room 208?
*
Why?
*
Well, that's unacceptable.
*
What am I going to do, stand here and argue? Jesus Christ.
(*Hangs up the phone*)
God forbid there's an emergency and our lives are entrusted with the twenty year old front desk dipshit. You have to go to the front desk for pillows.

BETH: What?

SAM: Housekeeper had to go to the hospital or something.

BETH: I think you need to go to the front desk, get me new pillows.

SAM: You can have one of my pillows.

BETH: I don't want your pillow.
(She gets her room key)

SAM: Hey, find out what happened to the housekeeper.

(BETH *exits*)

SAM: She's so moody. Killer prom night huh?

JONATHAN: Yeah.

SAM: How was your prom night, Ang?

ANGIE: It was nice. The theme was Moonlight Rendezvous. I went with a friend. We stayed up all night talking about the ethics of sentient robots.

JONATHAN: Like Asimov and stuff?

ANGIE: You like Asimov?

JONATHAN: Yeah.

SAM: *(To* JONATHAN, *re: cognac)* You good on that, want more?

JONATHAN: I'm good.

(Off SAM's *look)*

JONATHAN: What?

SAM: You and Beth.
Beth is what we call a "Slamlocker." Gets to the hotel, slams the door and locks it. Then every once in a while she'll pull a surprise. Like, one morning after a night in Alburquerque, Beth doesn't meet me for the cab. Called her room, no answer. Banged on her door, no answer. I think she's dead. Then Beth comes walking up from outside, covered in dirt. "I went to the desert. Do you have any Neosporin?" No further explanation.

JONATHAN: Where does Beth live?

ANGIE: Saint Louis.

SAM: We all live in Saint Louis. Well—

ANGIE: (*"Well" overlaps* SAM's *"well"*)
Well…I live in LaGrange.

SAM: Sorry things didn't work out with your hot prom date.

(JONATHAN *shrugs.*)

SAM: In twenty years, she'll go from hot to "pretty for her age." Disillusioned, disappointed, divorced. Wondering what happened to that nice guy she dumped on prom night. Her loss.

JONATHAN: She was really into my ear. With her tongue.

SAM: Oh yeah?

JONATHAN: She was like—nevermind.

SAM: Like what?

JONATHAN: I don't know.

SAM: Like what?

…

Like…

(*She licks his ear. Slow, seductive. It is punctuated with a bite to the earlobe.*)

(ANGIE *is just sippin cognac and watching.*)

(JONATHAN *tries to wipe her spit from his ear, but* SAM *grabs his wrist to stop his faux pas*)

SAM: No, no.

(JONATHAN *remembers* ANGIE *is there. He looks at her. She smiles at him.*)

(*The door opens.* SAM *releases* JONATHAN's *arm.* BETH *enters with the pillows.*)

BETH: The housekeeper is okay. Mildly electrocuted by a lamp, apparently.

ANGIE: I got electrocuted on a lamp once.

SAM: Really?

ANGIE: This arm still tingles before it rains.

JONATHAN: That's cool. You have a super power.

ANGIE: Never thought of it like that.

SAM: I am officially ready to hear how you two met.

BETH: We met last year. February I think. March?

JONATHAN: February.

BETH: This was back when...

(SAM *pours the remaining Sprite into her cognac, savoring* BETH's *silent disapproval*)

BETH: Back when they let Greg have a drug dog. They don't let Greg have a drug dog anymore but that's another story. He went through a whole ton of training to have a dog. Was all he ever wanted to talk about, working with drug dogs. And his favorite dog, Gertie, German Shepherd. Greg and Gertie. (*To* JONATHAN) Well you met Gertie.

JONATHAN: Gertie wanted to chomp my balls.

BETH: So Jonathan was in line to check bags. And your dad was there, right? That was your dad.

JONATHAN: Yeah.

BETH: And Greg's doing a casual patrol with Gertie. And Captain Genius here had half an ounce of ziplocked pot in his underwear. And there's Greg on the end of the—what is that?—it's like a leash but it's a guide dog bar? You know what I'm talking about. Not a leash, but a...

ALL: It's like a leash.... I don't know... "blind bar"?

BETH: Gertie goes nuts at Jonathan's, well, nuts.

JONATHAN: Nuts at my nuts.

BETH: You were terrified.

JONATHAN: It was a German Shepherd! They use those dogs in prisons!

BETH: I remember your dad now, and he was like.
(Imitates same fear-look)
And I was walking by the check-in on the way to security, late, walking fast. But I knew what that dog was after. I should've kept going.

JONATHAN: You didn't.

BETH: Well—I knew Greg with the dog and I was like "Greg! Hi!" And he's all—
(Mimes pulling on Gertie's dog guide leash)
"Oh hi Beth!" yanking. And I'm pretending I have no idea Gertie's got the sniff on Jonathan and I'm like "Haven't seen you in forever, Greg." True: I hadn't. And he's still with the dog on the guide like "Hold on, Beth? And I'm like "Can't, I'm late" And I was. Truth. And he was all "Wh—wait!" Yanks Gertie like a giant stuffed animal carnival prize toward me. And that's something, dragging a German Shepherd. Greg pulled Gertie away from Jonathan after I said "hi" to him. I'm like, "you're going after that kid? That kid." Said to Greg next time I'm in Denver, we'll have a drink. And then Jonathan was on my flight, Denver to O'Hare. Empty flight. Third full, max. We had an aside by the lavatories. That was that. Not much else to say about it.

SAM: Happily ever after.

JONATHAN: I guess.

BETH: God, that dog was huge. Well, you know how those dogs are Angie. You have that German Shepherd, right?

ANGIE: Oh, yeah.

BETH: How's he?

ANGIE: The vet put him down last week.

SAM: Anybody want more cognac?

BETH: What happened?

ANGIE: Tumor on his adrenal gland. The whites of his
eyes bulging out. Looked like someone was squeezing
him too hard.
The internal stuff, you can't see it. What's wrong on the
inside, who knows. But when the eyes go?
Bodies are such shit in the end.

(Silence)

BETH: Sorry about your dog, Ang.

JONATHAN: Yeah.

ANGIE: Thanks. Thanks. Sorry. Sidebar, right?

(Silence)

SAM: *(To* JONATHAN*)* Your parents know you, uh
(Gestures to BETH, *winks)*

BETH: Sam.

SAM: Just curious.
You wonder about who your child spends his time
with when he's not home. Isn't that something you
thought about, Ang? Before they were grown and gone
I'm saying.

ANGIE: Oh, sure, sometimes.

SAM: Like your kids are, what?

ANGIE: Annie's in, she's teaching in Austin. Jack is in,
uh. Last I heard? Was Portland. He doesn't, really –

SAM: My son doesn't tell me anything either, I mean…

ANGIE: Yeah.

SAM: I'm convinced he doesn't know anybody but his two slob friends who play shoot-'em-up zombie video games in the basement. And I know I'm not home a lot of the time, but that's my job, it's not me. So what I'm saying, I think, is do your mother a favor and tell her things occasionally. She'll appreciate it.

JONATHAN: I can't. She died last year.

SAM: Oh—oh.

(SAM *looks to* BETH *for confirmation. This is news to Beth too*)

Jesus. I'm really sorry.

ANGIE: Sorry to hear.

SAM: What…may I ask what…?

JONATHAN: Car accident. Drunk driver.

SAM: Oh Jesus. God, how awful. That's just so sad.

ANGIE: Real sad.

JONATHAN: I'm just going to go use the bathroom, okay?

BETH: Oh yeah.

(JONATHAN *exits into the bathroom*)

SAM: Thanks for making me feel like a fucking idiot.

BETH: What did I do?

SAM: You could've warned me not to bring up his dead mom.

BETH: I didn't know.

SAM: What exactly do you talk about when you're in the same room with somebody?

BETH: Tonight's the first night I've spent more than 5 minutes with him and if he wanted to talk about his mom, he would've brought it up, yeah?

SAM: Anything else I should know? Is his father still alive?

BETH: Yeah.

SAM: I don't like the taste of foot in my mouth after I step in shit.

(JONATHAN *enters from the bathroom.* SAM *hugs him.*)

SAM: Sweetheart, I'm so sorry for your loss. I am so, so sorry.

JONATHAN: Thanks.

SAM: You doing okay?

JONATHAN: Yeah. I'm all right. Thanks.

(*Silence*)

ANGIE: How much do you charge for an eighth?

JONATHAN: Depends on what you want.

ANGIE: What's Beth get?

JONATHAN: The good stuff.

ANGIE: (*To* BETH) Is it good?

BETH: Yep.

ANGIE: How much?

JONATHAN: Ninety for an eighth.

ANGIE: For an eighth? Sticker shock, that's for sure.

SAM: Wait. Did this turn into a drug deal?

ANGIE: Yes.

SAM: His mother died.

ANGIE: Would this be okay with your mom?

JONATHAN: Yeah.

BETH: You wouldn't have the good stuff on you tonight, right?

JONATHAN: I have a couple buds of some not-as-good stuff, but. You can think about it.

BETH: Sleep on it.

JONATHAN: Yeah, sleep on it.

SAM: Am I the only one in this room who cares about— *(Has forgotten his name)* —this…young man?

BETH: You forgot his name.

SAM: James. James?

BETH: James Bond? Were you thinking of James Bond?

(JONATHAN gets paper, pen. Writes his phone number. He gives the paper to ANGIE.)

JONATHAN: I can give you my phone number if you want to text me.

(SAM swipes the paper out of ANGIE's hand.)

ANGIE: Oh come on.

SAM: This is ridiculous.

ANGIE: Give me the paper.

SAM: You want the paper? You want the paper? *(She makes a show of crumpling the paper, putting it her mouth, chewing it.)*

(They watch SAM chew the paper.)

(JONATHAN gets another piece of paper and writes his phone number again to give to ANGIE. SAM will spit out the paper.)

SAM: Smoke yourself into the ground. Drink til your liver melts. I don't care. I really don't.
How much is an eighth of an ounce of marijuana?

BETH: Baggie this size.
(Gestures baggie size)

SAM: Ninety dollars for that…?
(Gestures)
Okay. Now I'm mad about the economics I don't
understand.
Do you know what I could buy for ninety dollars from
J Crew?

BETH: I'm dying to know what shitty pea coat you can
get from J Crew.

SAM: Pea coats cost more than ninety.
I'm talking more like a cute cardigan.

ANGIE: How much for the bud you have on you, like a
joint?

JONATHAN: Fifteen.

ANGIE: You have papers?

JONATHAN: Yeah.

ANGIE: Sold.

*(JONATHAN gets the pot and rolling paper from his bag,
ANGIE will get money from her purse)*

JONATHAN: Want me to roll it?

BETH: Rolls 'em nice.

ANGIE: Oh. Yes, please. Thank you.

SAM: Roll one for me.

JONATHAN: Seriously?

SAM: Seriously.

BETH: You know what time we have to be out.

SAM: I know the schedule.

*(JONATHAN looks to BETH. She shrugs. He will work on the
joints)*

SAM: Ang's got one thing going for her. She's already
been fired. The funny thing is you're more likely to get

fired for gaining a few pounds than for smoking dope.
So why not? You manage.

BETH: It's for my back. I'm in a lot of pain. It helps me
sleep.

SAM: Think you're going to win a medal for holding
out, not seeing a doctor? They don't give medals for
that. I should get a medal for listening you moan about
your back all the time. You got insurance. Use it. Use it
before something happens.

BETH: Like what.

SAM: Like you get fired?

BETH: I'm not going to get fired. I'm taking the
package.

SAM: Whoa. Wait. Hold on.

You're retiring?

BETH: It's a good package.

SAM: No it's not.

BETH: It's an all right package.

SAM: They cut *a month* off the guaranteed pay from the
last offer.

BETH: The insurance is still…

SAM: And the next time they offer, bam!, a month off
insurance.

BETH: You don't know that. You hear that from
somebody?

SAM: Every offer is lower than the last offer. And if you
quit, Beth, what are you going to do?

BETH: I don't know yet.

ANGIE: You can do anything. That's the hard part. The
anything part. I take care of my mom, that's every day.
Cook, clean. That's every day. Helping out her next

door neighbor too. Do her some shopping, cleaning.
(Thinks) You know what I miss? Sleeping in hotels.
Always slept like a baby in a hotel room. The same-
ness of each one. Like a bland hug. I don't sleep so well
anymore. I just don't sleep so well anymore.

SAM: You can't just...quit without a plan. What's out
there? Not a whole lot for us.

JONATHAN: She has a plan. She has a good plan.

SAM: Really.

JONATHAN: Yeah.

SAM: What's the big plan?

JONATHAN: She's going to start a microbrewery.

SAM: A microbrewery. *(To* BETH*)* A microbrewery?

BETH: I was smoking pot.

SAM: You were ah
(Gestures "smoking")
where good ideas are born.

JONATHAN: I'm going to design the labels for the
bottles.

*(*JONATHAN *gets his sketchbook.* SAM *looks over his shoulder
at the book)*

SAM: So you're going to retire and start a microbrewery
and he's going to design the labels?

BETH: We were just talking.

SAM: Well, why not? When I retire I'm going to
raise unicorns to plow fields of gum drops and
marshmallows.
(Looking at sketch)
What's that?

JONATHAN: An octopus.

SAM: Oh. Weird.

JONATHAN: It's okay if you don't like it.

ANGIE: Can I see?

SAM: I like it! I do. Really, sweetheart. It's great. And your microbrewery idea, Beth. Really great. A-plus awesome.

BETH: Yeah, yeah. Thanks for that.

SAM: I'm teasing, you know.

BETH: It's an idea.

SAM: I know! Beth. I'm sorry. I didn't realize you were serious about a microbrewery.

BETH: I'm not.
I wasn't serious.
It was just a thought. Just a thought I had once.

(JONATHAN *gives a joint to* ANGIE.)

JONATHAN: Here you go.

ANGIE: Thanks. Fifteen?

JONATHAN: Yeah.

(ANGIE *gets money from her purse.*)

SAM: You know, I might be a little low on cash for my joint. Especially if I'm getting the cab tomorrow.

JONATHAN: Okay?

SAM: I'm sure I have cash in my room, I'm sure.

JONATHAN: Okay.

SAM: But if I didn't have cash, we could work something out, right?

JONATHAN: What do you mean?

SAM: Oh, I don't know, I probably have cash, but if not, maybe I have something else you'd take.

JONATHAN: Okay.

SAM: Did you leave anything in my room? Angie?

ANGIE: Huh.

SAM: Did you leave anything in my room?

ANGIE: Um. ...I have my purse. My coat? My coat's in your room.

SAM: *(To* JONATHAN*)* How 'bout come over to my room. You can get your cash for the pot. And when you come back here, you bring Angie's coat.

BETH: How about you go get the cash from your room and bring back Angie's coat yourself?

SAM: Mmm. No. I don't want to do that.

BETH: I think that would be best.

JONATHAN: I don't mind.

BETH: You don't have to go to her room.

SAM: I'm not sure what difference it would make to you, Beth. Does it make a difference he comes over to my room a few minutes?

(Pause)

BETH: I suppose not.

(Pause)

SAM: Angie. Hey Ang.

ANGIE: Yeah.

SAM: I'll send James Bond on a return mission with your coat. So. I don't know when I'll see you next.

ANGIE: You're leaving?

SAM: Yeah.

ANGIE: It was great seeing you, Sam. I missed you.

SAM: Missed you too.

ANGIE: Glad we could do this, get together, like.

SAM: Take care of yourself, all right?

ANGIE: I'll try.

SAM: *(To* BETH*)* Five-thirty.

*(*SAM *opens the door for* JONATHAN, *follows him out, door shuts.)*

ANGIE: She's going to eat that boy alive.

BETH: Oh god.

ANGIE: Good ol' Sam. Some people never change.
(She will put the joint between her lips—just a place to hold it to free her hands as she flips through JONATHAN*'s sketchbook)*
He's very talented.

BETH: Yeah.

ANGIE: *(Finds the naked lady sketches)* Va va voom.

BETH: You want to smoke? I can take you outside.

ANGIE: Save it for tomorrow. After mom goes to bed. Sit in the backyard, then hit the sky, then hit the ground, maybe a combination of the two.
(She tucks the joint behind her ear.)
Something to look forward to.

BETH: You're gonna lose it there.

ANGIE: It stays put, see.
(Shakes her head to prove it won't fall out)

BETH: Here.

*(*BETH *takes the joint from behind* ANGIE*'s ear and wraps up in plastic from the cups, hands it to* ANGIE*)*

BETH: Put it in your purse so you remember you put it in your purse. Muscle memory.

ANGIE: I'll put it in with the reading glasses. So it doesn't get crushed.

BETH: Good thinking.

(ANGIE *puts it in her glasses case.*)

BETH: You'll remember you put it in there?

ANGIE: I'll remember.
(She takes out her car keys.)

BETH: Let's watch TV for a little.

ANGIE: What's on?

BETH: Saturday Night Live maybe.

ANGIE: Who's hosting.

BETH: Don't know.

ANGIE: That'll be good.

BETH: *(Gestures to the bed)* Go on.

(ANGIE *sits on the bed.* BETH *will turn on the T V.* BETH *sits on the bed with* ANGIE. *Their comfort with each other is mutual.)*

BETH: Sam mentioned your divorce went through?

ANGIE: Long time coming.

BETH: I didn't even know you were in Chicago.

ANGIE: Southwest suburbs. Closer to Midway.

*(*BETH *flips the T V channel)*

ANGIE: I used to remember what hotels had what channels and what T V shows were on at what time in what city and that's how I would know where I was. Like a bird flying on the blips and static of electric waves and never finding a place to land but always always always knowing when Jeopardy is on. I'll take Potent Potables for one thousand.
(Drinks)

(A knock at the door)

(BETH *and* ANGIE *look at their watches.)*

(BETH *gets up, opens the door.)*

(JONATHAN *is there. His tie is undone, shirt untucked.*)

(*He is agitated. Gets his backpack preparing to leave for good*)

BETH: What happened?

JONATHAN: Nothing.

BETH: Nothing? Where are you going?

JONATHAN: I gotta go.

BETH: Go where, where are you going.

JONATHAN: I'm going home.

BETH: Hold on, what happened?

JONATHAN: I'm going home I don't know what I'm doing here. Why doesn't anybody want me?!
(*He punches the wall in frustration. He hurts his hand badly*)

ANGIE: Oh.

JONATHAN: AAAAAOWWW!

BETH: Go into the bathroom—

JONATHAN: Leave me alone.

BETH: Go into the bathroom, count to a hundred.

(JONATHAN *tries to get by* BETH *to leave the room.*)

BETH: GO INTO THE BATHROOM AND COUNT TO A HUNDRED

JONATHAN: FINE (Jesuschrist)
(*He goes into the bathroom and slams the door.*)

(BETH *picks up the phone, dials.*)

(ANGIE *will get the ice bucket and go to the closed bathroom door.*)

BETH: (*On phone:*) What did you do?
*
Yeah he's here, why did you kick him out?

(ANGIE *taps on the bathroom door.*)

JONATHAN: *(Behind door)* WHAT!

ANGIE: Hi, it's Angie. Do you want some ice for your hand?

BETH: *(On phone:)* Okay. Well.
*

You know what time we have to be out.

(JONATHAN *opens the bathroom door*)

ANGIE: Was that your drawing hand?

(It was. JONATHAN *flexes it a few times.)*

ANGIE: Here.

JONATHAN: Naw, I'm fine.

ANGIE: It'll help.

(JONATHAN *allows* ANGIE *to ease his hand into the ice.*)

BETH: *(On phone:)* Sam, listen to me, all right? Don't smoke it in the room. Go 'round the back.
*

Through the parking lot and…yeah.
*

Don't get lost.
(She hangs up the phone)
She said she changed her mind.

JONATHAN: Oh.
Okay.
(Re: his hand in the ice)
This is really cold.
(He begins crying. It's quiet and hardly seems like crying at all until he wipes his eyes with his hand)

BETH: Do you want me to see if your porn movie is still playing on the pay-per-view?

JONATHAN: No.

(Pause)

ANGIE: I like your drawings. Did you teach yourself, or…?

JONATHAN: I don't know.

ANGIE: I bet people ask you to draw them stuff all the time.

JONATHAN: They don't.

ANGIE: They will. You're very good.

*(*JONATHAN *picks up his sketch pad, pen.)*

*(*BETH *eases herself back onto the bed. Her back is bothering her again. At some point,* JONATHAN *will take his hand out of the ice and draw in his sketch pad. He will remain present in the room, listening, drawing.)*

ANGIE: Promise you'll do something about your back.

BETH: Why?

ANGIE: If you're in pain you should do something about it.

BETH: You know how I fucked it up, right? After that Christmas flight? The last flight we worked together. When I slipped on that coffee in the terminal at Lambert.

ANGIE: That did it.

BETH: It's not even a good story. It would be one thing if all this pain came out of some heroic event… but it's just boring.

Merry Christmas to me. Back problems for life.

ANGIE: Do you remember the woman on that Christmas flight, last one off the plane because she was waiting for the wheelchair service to get to the gate? Older woman in the holiday sweater with the snowflakes. And she was so worried about her luggage.

BETH: Vaguely.

ANGIE: She was the one who gave me this bottle of cognac.

BETH: Really? That's a helluva gift.

ANGIE: Yeah. Yeah.

After you slipped on the coffee and walked off in a cloud of curse words to the Metrolink, I saw her at baggage claim. Andy was supposed to pick me up but I got a voicemail and he was like… "I'm just not going to be home."

And so I was going to take a cab home. And the woman in the deep red Snowflake sweater is sitting in her wheelchair. She's at the belt and she's dismissed her handler. She is alone. She is watching a single suitcase go around. And around. And around. And I stand watching this woman watch her bag. She sees me, and she sees my uniform, and she recognizes me from her flight. And she asks, pointing to the bag as it makes its way around, "Can you help me, please?"

I pull her bag from the belt. An old, navy blue Samsonite. Too large for whatever was inside. It was so light I almost flung it across baggage claim as I picked it up. And she thought I was so kind to her on the flight and now helping her with her bag, and I said I'm happy to help. And she said she didn't live far from the airport and asked, would I like to come over to her house for a Christmas drink. I didn't want to be alone on Christmas, you know?

She makes a call in the cab, calls the nurse who's been at her house caring for her husband. He's a former law professor at Wash U, dying of pancreatic cancer. She says to the nurse she'll be home shortly and to go home and have a Merry Christmas. Ends the call. I ask, "what were you doing in San Francisco?" to make small talk. She tells me she had just been in San Francisco to

visit a friend who knew a man who, it turns out, sells
morphine. And to that fact I say... "Oh." And I have a
very bad feeling, and I want to throw myself out of the
cab to get away from this very nice woman.
Her home is nice, comfortable. Wreath on the door, tree
in the living room. And the woman in the Snowflake
sweater asks if I like cognac...
(She holds up the bottle.)
Cracks the seal. Pours. We sip. She asks me about what
it's like to travel everywhere and do I enjoy my work,
and I am afraid to ask her a single question in the 45
minutes we sit in her living room. I give a glance of
the watch and say I should be going, and she insists
on giving me cash to pay for the cab home. She leaves
to get the money. And she's gone for a bit. I think,
maybe she's forgotten about me and I should call my
cab and go. But she returns with an envelope and she
says, "You have been so kind. I would be grateful if
you could stay one more hour. Stay downstairs and
watch T V if you'd like. I have to take care of my
husband upstairs. It would help to know someone was
downstairs. To know that someone was in the house
with me for the next hour. I won't come downstairs.
I would be grateful for your company. Here's some
money for your ride home."
And in the envelope, there's a thousand dollars, cash.
And I said...okay.
She gets a zip-up leather pouch, about this big *(Gestures
the size)*, from her very empty navy blue Samsonite,
and I pour myself more cognac, and she goes upstairs.
I listen to the sound of the house and for any noise
upstairs. An hour passes. I'm going to call upstairs for
the woman in the snowflake sweater to tell her I'm
leaving, and I can't shout her name because I don't
know her name.

I walk to the top of the stairs and, like. The temperature
drops. The hallway is dark. There's the door to a
bedroom at the end of the hallway that's slightly open,
yellow light spilling into the hallway. The top of the
stairs is as far as I go because I knew—
I knew.
I didn't need to see it.
As long as I didn't look...
Called a cab.
Put the bottle of cognac in my bag.
Let myself out.
I went home. Andy had cleared out his closet.
I drank the cognac and I drank it until I threw it up
and I'm fucking pissed I threw up this very expensive
cognac, you know? Even as it was coming out of me I
was thinking "this is really expensive vomit."
I'm sorry I took her cognac. I put the bottle in the trunk
of my car and I was going to return it to her house, but.
I should have looked in her room, with her husband, to
see.
I should have helped or called somebody.
I should have done something.

BETH: You did do something.

ANGIE: What?

BETH: You were the person who was there.

(BETH *makes a comforting, physical gesture toward* ANGIE.)

ANGIE: Wish I still had my job.
Wish I could see everybody again.
All the people I used to talk to at the airport, on the
airplane. Even the passengers who weren't very nice.
And the people who weren't anything but sitting there,
reading a magazine, going some place. And that one
janitor in Saint Louis who called me "sugar". You
know who I'm talking about?

BETH: Yeah.

ANGIE: He called everybody "sugar", and it seemed like he really meant it. What a nice man.

(BETH *sits with* ANGIE *as she falls asleep.* BETH *turns off the T V.*)

BETH: Hey. Hey.

ANGIE: *(Sleepy)* Mm?

BETH: Scooch.

(BETH *helps* ANGIE *scooch down into the bed to get comfortable and sleep.* BETH *takes off* ANGIE*'s shoes. Covers her with the sheet, blanket)*

BETH: *(To* JONATHAN*)* I have to get Sam.

JONATHAN: *(Looks up from his work)* I'm sorry what?

BETH: I have to get Sam. She's outside and she's not very good at drugs.

JONATHAN: Is it okay if I stay and finish this?

BETH: Um.

JONATHAN: I'll be quiet.

BETH: Sure. Yeah. Sure.

(JONATHAN *returns to his work.* BETH *puts on her jacket, goes to the door. She looks back at him, busy, unaware of her departure.)*

BETH: *(To herself)* All right.

(BETH *exits.* ANGIE *wakes at the sound of the door shutting. She looks at* JONATHAN.*)*

ANGIE: How's your hand?

(JONATHAN *looks at his hand, flexes it,)*

JONATHAN: I punched a wall.

ANGIE: Yeah you did.

(JONATHAN *shows* ANGIE *the drawing in progress.)*

ANGIE: That's fantastic.

JONATHAN: *(Resumes drawing)* It's for you.

(A moment. ANGIE closes her eyes, ready to sleep.)

Scene Four

(Behind the hotel. SAM smokes the joint. Noise of an approaching airplane. Louder and louder)

(BETH enters.)

(They look up. A huge noise. Then it goes.)

SAM: Did you see that?

BETH: The giant loud airplane?

SAM: Did you see it?

BETH: It was pretty giant and loud.

SAM: It's scary back here. I saw a bear.

BETH: There are no bears.

SAM: You don't know that. This is nature. This is kill or
be killed wilderness.
Maybe it was a bush a bear-shaped bush.
Here's what's happening: Tomorrow. I'm going to fly
to Paris. Paris, France. I'm going to be a Paris-person.

BETH: Parisian.

SAM: A Parisian Paris Person in Paris. Work on my
French. Ou est la piscine…where is the swimming
pool.

BETH: You need to go to bed.

(SAM smokes.)

BETH: Sam.
Sam.
Sam.

SAM: What.

BETH: I have to work with you at five-thirty and you have to be semi-somewhat functional.

SAM: I'm calling in sick.

BETH: No.

SAM: Plenty a people in Chicago be happy to pick up my hours.

BETH: You're going to work.

SAM: I'm doing you a favor, Beth. You don't like working with me. You don't have to work with me. Asshole.

BETH: Give me the joint.

SAM: You're an asshole to me, you're an asshole to Angie.

BETH: To Angie?

SAM: You know how hurt she was when I told her you didn't want to come out to Cotters Lounge tonight? She just wanted to spend a couple hours with her old friend. Her old friend who never once bothered to call her after she got fired. You have no right to get indignant over how I treat people. You think I treat people badly? Take a look at yourself.

(JONATHAN *enters.*)

JONATHAN: You forgot your room key.

(JONATHAN *gives room key to* BETH.)

BETH: Thanks.

JONATHAN: I think I'm leaving.
(*To* SAM:)
You, uh…

(SAM *smokes.*)

JONATHAN: You owe me for the pot.

You didn't pay me.

SAM: Look, James—

JONATHAN: Jonathan.

SAM: Ohh *(Shit)* What happened was I got a text from my, uh…I had to deal with something at home. Is why I kicked you out of my room. If things got confused… or…whatever. That's what happened.

JONATHAN: I didn't want to do it with you anyway.

(A moment)

SAM: Didn't want to do it with me.
Did you just dump me?
He dumped me.
Sweetheart…

JONATHAN: Don't call me that.

SAM: Okay. Fine. This broken heart will mend with time.

JONATHAN: Stop making fun of me.

SAM: *(Dropping it. Serious)* We were screwing around. You're stuck somewhere you don't want to be and you screw around. That's what happens. No big deal.
No big deal.

JONATHAN: Yeah okay.
But.
You still owe me money for the pot.

(SAM nods. She cries. JONATHAN looks to BETH for help,)

BETH: Sam.

SAM: Oh god. Get this away from me.

(BETH takes SAM's joint.)

BETH: What's going on at home?

SAM: It's T.J.

(She gets her phone out)
He texted me a photo.

(SAM shows BETH the photo.)

BETH: I don't know what I'm looking at.

SAM: *(Tearfully)* He cleaned the kitchen.

BETH: Okay?

SAM: It's not even that clean when I'm home.

BETH: But everything's okay with T.J.

SAM: He's great.

(Pause)

BETH: You gonna be okay for work?

SAM: Yeah.

BETH: You still okay calling the cab?

SAM: Yeah.

BETH: You sure?

SAM: No.

BETH: I'll call.

SAM: I've got cash but if you can call.

BETH: It will be done.

SAM: I'm…
I'm…
I'm going to bed.

BETH: Five-thirty.

SAM: Five-thirty.
(She walks the wrong direction)

BETH: That way.

SAM: I know!
(She goes the other, correct way, exiting.)

BETH: *(Re:* JONATHAN'*s untied bowtie)*
This is driving me crazy.

JONATHAN: What?

BETH: Untied ties drive me crazy.

(JONATHAN *adjusts the lengths and makes the first cross-over. That's as far as he knows)*

BETH: Oh, Jesus Christ.

JONATHAN: I don't know, my dad tied it for me.

BETH: Here.

(BETH *will tie* JONATHAN'*s bow tie.)*

JONATHAN: You know how to tie it?

BETH: My mom taught me. She said it was a woman's responsibility to make sure her man looks presentable. You need to learn how to tie a tie.

JONATHAN: Now?

BETH: I can't teach you without a mirror. Promise you'll learn.

JONATHAN: Yeah okay.

BETH: I tied a bow tie for a passenger once. Twenty-something year old guy, dressed up to propose to his girlfriend when he got to Syracuse. He went into the toilet with the broken latch. We hit turbulence, and he was thrown backwards through the door with his dick in his hands, spraying a fountain of piss. Other than that, he looked fantastic, with his tie tied perfectly.
(She finishes the tie)
Tuck in your shirt.

(JONATHAN *does.* BETH *dusts something off his shoulder.)*

BETH: How much we still owe you for the pot?

JONATHAN: You owe nine dollars. Sam owes fifteen.

BETH: We're terrible customers.

JONATHAN: You're, like, worse than freshmen.

BETH: Give me your address so I can send you the money.

JONATHAN: Well if I'm gonna see you next-next week—

BETH: Give me your address.

JONATHAN: Yeah. Okay.
(He gets his sketch book, writes his address on the back of one of the sketches. Tears it out)

BETH: You don't have to give me your gorgeous tentacles.
(A moment, looking at the drawing)
I'll send you those old comic books I mentioned. The Wally Wood stuff. They just sit in an old box. I don't need them. I mean I'll keep some of them, but there's a lot. They're not worth much. Most of them are well-read, creases in the pages, rips. The art is good.

JONATHAN: Can I tell you something?

BETH: All right.

JONATHAN: You were my first.

BETH: First…first what? I'm sorry what?

JONATHAN: You were the first person I sold pot to.

BETH: Ever?

JONATHAN: Yeah.

BETH: You're kidding.

JONATHAN: The pot the dog in Denver sniffed? I got that pot from my hippie ski bum uncle in Boulder who gave it to me after my mom's funeral. "For the rough times, man." Then you were looking to buy and I thought, I oughta figure out how to get more if she ever really does call me.

BETH: Well shit.

JONATHAN: What?

BETH: I wish you hadn't told me that.

JONATHAN: Why not?

BETH: I thought you knew what you were doing.

JONATHAN: I thought *you* knew what *you* were doing.

BETH: I didn't know what I was doing.

JONATHAN: Me neither.

BETH: Well shit.

JONATHAN: It's cool.

BETH: No it is not cool.

JONATHAN: Nah, it's cool, 'cuz we didn't know what we were doing at the same time and we're both here and neither one of us have been arrested. High five.

(JONATHAN *holds up hand for high five.* BETH *is not in a high five mood.)*

JONATHAN: Beth, I would have been screwed if you hadn't helped me in Denver. And once I started selling at school, I was the guy people wanted to know. Like, I got some respect. Like, my prom date Molly. Do you think she would have gone out with me if I didn't help her friends get high? No way. She was way too pretty to date me under normal circumstances. So that part of dealing has been great but one time I got punched, like, in the side of the head. That's why I carry a knife. Like. Just in case.
(Pause)
Am I going to see you again?
(Pause)

BETH: I don't think we should do this anymore.
(Pause)

You shouldn't be selling drugs. You shouldn't be
getting punched in the head. You shouldn't carry a
knife.

JONATHAN: I'll be all right.

BETH: You could get really hurt.

JONATHAN: What am I supposed to do?

BETH: I don't know.

JONATHAN: Quit?

BETH: I don't know.

JONATHAN: Stop?

BETH: I don't know!
You have no idea how good a person you are. That
kills me. You have no idea.
Get out of here. Go to Caltech. You'll do great out
there.

JONATHAN: I can't.

BETH: You can.

JONATHAN: No. I can't, Beth.
My dad…I don't know if he'll be okay if I move away.
Like…
He's alone. He drinks a lot. He…
He's really alone.
You know?

BETH: I know…it's not easy.

*(A distant sound of an airplane. [*The noise will get louder
and louder, climaxing at the end of the play*])*

BETH: *(Pause)* If I, uh.
I'm not saying I will.
But if I did start a—
Were you serious about drawing labels for me?

JONATHAN: Yeah.

BETH: We'd stay in touch about you drawing something for me.

JONATHAN: I'd like that.

BETH: Okay.

Okay.

I'd like that too.

(Pause)

I know nothing about brewing beer.

I have *a* book.

JONATHAN: *A* book is one more book than *no* books.

BETH: It's from the library and it's overdue.

JONATHAN: Maybe it's overdue because deep down you wanted to keep it and read it.

BETH: Maybe deep down I wanna strangle you.

I'm not quitting my job. I can't quit.

JONATHAN: What about the retirement package?

BETH: It's a shit package. It would float me a year.

I'm a flight attendant. I'm good at it. It's a job, which is a lot more than most people have.

It would be insane to start something new.

(BETH and JONATHAN both have to shout over the airplane noise now.)

JONATHAN: Yeah but let's get started anyway.

BETH: Get started? I have to go to bed!

JONATHAN: It's not that late! We'll get started.

BETH: I can't—

(Gestures "can't hear")

JONATHAN: You just gotta do it. It'll be awesome.

BETH: "Awesome."

JONATHAN: *(Gestures "Can't hear")* Hold on.

Hold on 'til this passes.

(The airplane screams overhead and BETH *and* JONATHAN
watch it go.)

END OF PLAY